Personalized Love Coupons

This Personalized Love Coupons Book Belongs To

_____

_____

Copyrights © The Little Gifts Shop

All Rights Reserved

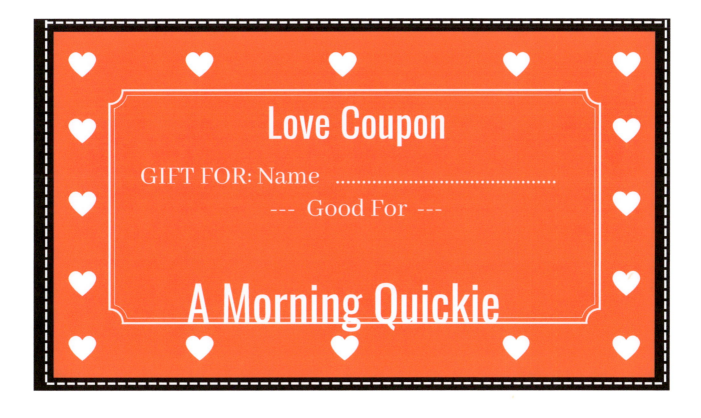

Love Coupon

GIFT FOR: Name ....

--- Good For ---

Join Me In The Shower

Love Coupon

GIFT FOR: Name ....

--- Good For ---

Romantic Candle Light Dinner

Thank You For Purchasing Our Personalized Love Coupons Book - We Really hope it brings you great fun and Love.

WE THRIVE ON YOUR REVIEWS! Please In Your Own Time Come Back With Your Honest Review Thanks Again & Enjoy!

www.ingramcontent.com/pod-product-compliance
Lightning Source LLC
LaVergne TN
LVHW072257120225

803630LV00025B/144